This Book belongs to

...A.N.N...MARIE...REYNOLDS...

'To keep me with you, sign your name,
or you may lose me through my fame.'

THE ORACLE

of
Madame Marie

Your Book of Fate

SOUVENIR PRESS

For
my children
Gillian, Christopher and Gregory

First published 1994 by
Souvenir Press Ltd,
43 Great Russell Street, London WC1B 3PA
and simultaneously in Canada

Reprinted 1996

ISBN 0 285 63231 0

Printed and bound in Great Britain by
Biddles Ltd, Guildford and King's Lynn

Introduction

From time immemorial, people faced with dilemmas, problems, the incalculability of other people or situations, or just plain curiosity about the future, have been drawn to divination, or fortune-telling. From the humble teacup (I have seen some amazing things in teacups) to the complex charts of the astrologer, the aim is the same: to ask a question of Fate — and to get an answer.

During my many years as a professional clairvoyant I have given readings to people from all walks of life, from sceptical scientists to superstitious theatre people; from doctors and lawyers to a sprinkling of aristocrats and many ordinary people. Behind their external differences, all human beings want to know remarkably similar things and suffer similar troubles. I have done my best to enlighten and help them, and continue to do so. There are times, however, when people wish to divine for themselves, in secrecy, or for some reason cannot consult a clairvoyant. It is for these occasions that this Oracle has been written.

In it I have combined the old and the new. The traditional layout of all Oracles, even in Victorian times, used a rondel beginning with the mystic number 5 and closing the circle at 100. Nobody now knows why this was done for the reasons are lost in antiquity, but it seems likely that the first four question numbers were omitted in order to guard the Oracle from mischief, the theory being that having tried to interfere four times imps would then desist! Whatever the reason, I have found no need to depart from the old layout.

What I have changed is the method of working the Oracle. The old systems were extremely complicated and time-consuming, especially to those who were unfamiliar with them, involving calculations and variables after each question, of such complexity that the reader could be forgiven for giving up after the first two or three answers, interesting though they might be.

I have therefore chosen to use dice as the method to unlock the wisdom of the Oracle. As you will see from the instructions below, this is simplicity itself. It can be mastered in a few minutes, and after that the Oracle is available and open at all times.

Although no method is foolproof, and fortune-telling should be regarded as an entertainment, not as a blueprint for life, when properly used and sincerely consulted the Oracle should give a high degree of accuracy. It is dependent upon the concentration of the questioner, the intuitive answers I have given, and the hand of Fate which governs the roll of the dice.

It must be said, however, that trickery brings its own reward. The Oracle is not mocked: a deliberately nonsensical question (for example, a question for a young person being asked by one already old) will receive a nonsensical reply, or even a refusal to answer at all — and your subsequent questions may also come to grief.

Let us assume that you are a serious questioner. To consult the Oracle through the mystical tables takes only a minute for each question. This is the procedure to follow:

1 Sit at a table with a shaker containing the two dice ready for use, and the book on your left.

2 Choose a *suitable* question from the list on pages xi-xiv, to which you sincerely wish to have an answer. Write down or memorise *the number of the question*.

3 Pick up the shaker and *concentrate* on your question, with your eyes closed, as you shake the dice.

4 At the moment of casting the dice on the table, *demand* silently that the answer shall be given to you. Open your eyes and note the total number on the upward-facing sides of the dice.

Now turn to the Mystical Tables on the pages following the questions. The *question numbers* are on the *left* in bold type. Run your finger down the column until you come to the number of the question you chose; then, keeping your finger on the same line, move it to the right, across the page, until it is directly underneath the number you cast with the dice. The number you are now touching indicates the *page* on which your answer can be found, and the number of the dice is the *position* on the page that you have to look for and read.

For example, if you chose question number 18, and threw a total of 9 on the dice, you would be directed to page number 75, where your answer would be waiting beside the 9 symbol:

[⚅ ⚂]

Once you have carried out this easy procedure, you will be able to follow it again and again. Remember, though, that you must throw the dice each time you ask a different question.

You will find that the dice numbers have been shown in the Mystical Tables, and on the pages of answers, as pairs of squares with dots. When you throw your dice, remember that it is the *total number* of the two dice that matters. Do not worry if your total of 9 is split 5 and 4 while the book shows 6 and 3:

[⚄ ⚃] = [⚅ ⚂]

There is no limit to the number of questions you can ask, but you should remember that it is not well to ask any question more than once in any day — even if you don't like the answer you are given! The powers of the Oracle are always greater by evening and night than during daylight hours, and it is especially fortunate to consult on a Tuesday.

I hope that my clients, for whom this book was originally compiled, and all other readers, will enjoy the Oracle.

Although it is yours to consult in privacy at any time, it can also be used in a family group or a gathering of friends, to tell fortunes on a lighter level. There is no need to be serious, only sincere, and provided the correct method is followed, there is no limit to the number who can take part. Simply sit round a table together, asking and answering only one question in turn, then passing the book to the person on your *left*. In a group it is more fun if people say what question they are asking, and read the answer aloud. You can continue like this indefinitely, taking turns.

Be sure you have the book returned to you at the end of the evening, or you may never get it back! It must be yours alone: write your name on the first page of this book, in the space provided, *as soon as you get it*, and do not give or lend it out of your possession, unless you have no further use for it. My intuition tells me that unsigned Oracles that go missing from their owners will not return.

Now it is time for you to turn to the next page and select your first question. Good luck!

The Oracle speaks!

for

the light prevails

and

The Children of Men

are bid

to make their

inquiries!

Questions

55 Will the news I am waiting for come soon?

56 Shall I do it?

57 Do my friends tell me everything?

58 Shall I inherit very much?

59 Shall I die single, married or widowed?

60 Shall I travel much more in my life?

61 Shall I have many burdens to bear?

62 What can I do about an ultimatum given to me by my partner?

63 What will happen if I am discovered in my deception?

64 Why does he prefer her to me?

65 Shall I live long?

66 Will my health be good?

67 Oracle, help me make a decision.

68 How much longer will my grief last?

69 Shall I ever be truly happy again?

70 If I keep the appointment, shall I be able to resist him?

71 Ought I to trust the promise that has been made to me?

72 Will he ever change for the better?

73 Ought I to confess all to the person I am thinking about?

74 How can I make them give me the explanation they owe me?

75 Have I anything to gain by fighting on?

76 Have I any rivals for his affections?

77 Ought I to challenge openly the person I am jealous of?

78 Shall I get what I want in the situation I am in?

79 What should I do about my money worries?

The Mystical Tables
1

Dice numbers correspond to answers on each page

Question number	⚀/⚀	⚁/⚁	⚂/⚂	⚃/⚃	⚄/⚄	⚅/⚀	⚅/⚁	⚅/⚂	⚅/⚃	⚅/⚄	⚅/⚅
5	20	26	32	38	44	50	56	62	68	74	80
6	21	27	33	39	45	51	57	63	69	75	81
7	22	28	34	40	46	52	58	64	70	76	82
8	23	29	35	41	47	53	59	65	71	77	83
9	24	30	36	42	48	54	60	66	72	78	84
10	25	31	37	43	49	55	61	67	73	79	85
11	26	32	38	44	50	56	62	68	74	80	86
12	27	33	39	45	51	57	63	69	75	81	87
13	28	34	40	46	52	58	64	70	76	82	88
14	29	35	41	47	53	59	65	71	77	83	89
15	30	36	42	48	54	60	66	72	78	84	90
16	31	37	43	49	55	61	67	73	79	85	91
17	32	38	44	50	56	62	68	74	80	86	92
18	33	39	45	51	57	63	69	75	81	87	93
19	34	40	46	52	58	64	70	76	82	88	94
20	35	41	47	53	59	65	71	77	83	89	95
21	36	42	48	54	60	66	72	78	84	90	96
22	37	43	49	55	61	67	73	79	85	91	97
23	38	44	50	56	62	68	74	80	86	92	98
24	39	45	51	57	63	69	75	81	87	93	99

The Mystical Tables

2

Dice numbers correspond to answers on each page

Question number	⚀	⚁	⚂	⚃	⚄	⚅				
25	40	46	52	58	64	70	76	82	88	94	100
26	41	47	53	59	65	71	77	83	89	95	5
27	42	48	54	60	66	72	78	84	90	96	6
28	43	49	55	61	67	73	79	85	91	97	7
29	44	50	56	62	68	74	80	86	92	98	8
30	45	51	57	63	69	75	81	87	93	99	9
31	46	52	58	64	70	76	82	88	94	100	10
32	47	53	59	65	71	77	83	89	95	5	11
33	48	54	60	66	72	78	84	90	96	6	12
34	49	55	61	67	73	79	85	91	97	7	13
35	50	56	62	68	74	80	86	92	98	8	14
36	51	57	63	69	75	81	87	93	99	9	15
37	52	58	64	70	76	82	88	94	100	10	16
38	53	59	65	71	77	83	89	95	5	11	17
39	54	60	66	72	78	84	90	96	6	12	18
40	55	61	67	73	79	85	91	97	7	13	19
41	56	62	68	74	80	86	92	98	8	14	20
42	57	63	69	75	81	87	93	99	9	15	21
43	58	64	70	76	82	88	94	100	10	16	22

The Mystical Tables

3

Dice numbers correspond to answers on each page

Question number											
44	59	65	71	77	83	89	95	5	11	17	23
45	60	66	72	78	84	90	96	6	12	18	24
46	61	67	73	79	85	91	97	7	13	19	25
47	62	68	74	80	86	92	98	8	14	20	26
48	63	69	75	81	87	93	99	9	15	21	27
49	64	70	76	82	88	94	100	10	16	22	28
50	65	71	77	83	89	95	5	11	17	23	29
51	66	72	78	84	90	96	6	12	18	24	30
52	67	73	79	85	91	97	7	13	19	25	31
53	68	74	80	86	92	98	8	14	20	26	32
54	69	75	81	87	93	99	9	15	21	27	33
55	70	76	82	88	94	100	10	16	22	28	34
56	71	77	83	89	95	5	11	17	23	29	35
57	72	78	84	90	96	6	12	18	24	30	36
58	73	79	85	91	97	7	13	19	25	31	37
59	74	80	86	92	98	8	14	20	26	32	38
60	75	81	87	93	99	9	15	21	27	33	39
61	76	82	88	94	100	10	16	22	28	34	40
62	77	83	89	95	5	11	17	23	29	35	41

The Mystical Tables
4

Dice numbers correspond to answers on each page

Question number

	⚀⚀	⚀⚁	⚀⚂	⚀⚃	⚀⚄	⚀⚅	⚁⚀	⚁⚁	⚁⚂	⚁⚃	⚁⚄
63	78	84	90	96	6	12	18	24	30	36	42
64	79	85	91	97	7	13	19	25	31	37	43
65	80	86	92	98	8	14	20	26	32	38	44
66	81	87	93	99	9	15	21	27	33	39	45
67	82	88	94	100	10	16	22	28	34	40	46
68	83	89	95	5	11	17	23	29	35	41	47
69	84	90	96	6	12	18	24	30	36	42	48
70	85	91	97	7	13	19	25	31	37	43	49
71	86	92	98	8	14	20	26	32	38	44	50
72	87	93	99	9	15	21	27	33	39	45	51
73	88	94	100	10	16	22	28	34	40	46	52
74	89	95	5	11	17	23	29	35	41	47	53
75	90	96	6	12	18	24	30	36	42	48	54
76	91	97	7	13	19	25	31	37	43	49	55
77	92	98	8	14	20	26	32	38	44	50	56
78	93	99	9	15	21	27	33	39	45	51	57
79	94	100	10	16	22	28	34	40	46	52	58
80	95	5	11	17	23	29	35	41	47	53	59
81	96	6	12	18	24	30	36	42	48	54	60

Dice numbers correspond to answers on each page

Question number	⚀⚀	⚁⚀	⚂⚁	⚃⚂	⚄⚃	⚅⚀	⚅⚁	⚅⚂	⚅⚃	⚅⚄	⚅⚅
82	97	7	13	19	25	31	37	43	49	55	61
83	98	8	14	20	26	32	38	44	50	56	62
84	99	9	15	21	27	33	39	45	51	57	63
85	100	10	16	22	28	34	40	46	52	58	64
86	5	11	17	23	29	35	41	47	53	59	65
87	6	12	18	24	30	36	42	48	54	60	66
88	7	13	19	25	31	37	43	49	55	61	67
89	8	14	20	26	32	38	44	50	56	62	68
90	9	15	21	27	33	39	45	51	57	63	69
91	10	16	22	28	34	40	46	52	58	64	70
92	11	17	23	29	35	41	47	53	59	65	71
93	12	18	24	30	36	42	48	54	60	66	72
94	13	19	25	31	37	43	49	55	61	67	73
95	14	20	26	32	38	44	50	56	62	68	74
96	15	21	27	33	39	45	51	57	63	69	75
97	16	22	28	34	40	46	52	58	64	70	76
98	17	23	29	35	41	47	53	59	65	71	77
99	18	24	30	36	42	48	54	60	66	72	78
100	19	25	31	37	43	49	55	61	67	73	79

The Oracle
Page 5

[1][1]	By a fortunate chance, you will.
[2][1]	By a twist of fate.
[2][2]	If they do not do it willingly, be sure it will be a tissue of lies.
[3][2]	It is falling behind you, and will soon be a thing of the past.
[3][3]	Surrender!
[5][1]	The Oracle stands aside. This must be your decision.
[5][2]	Keep a sharp eye open for opportunities in work or business.
[5][3]	She is a little jealous, as are you of her, but no more.
[5][4]	Your occupation is but a stepping stone to another, infinitely more glorious!
[5][5]	Only by the uninitiated!
[5][5]	Yes: make sure you repay the friendship, in full.

⚀ ⚀ It is best to do nothing. Tiptoe away.

⚁ ⚀ What was the question?

⚁ ⚁ Yes — victory, says the Oracle!

⚂ ⚂ All things new are lucky signs for you now: new house, new baby . . . new anything: these omens show you journeying back to happiness.

⚃ ⚃ Nobody but yourself is deceived, my dear!

⚅ ⚀ They are too canny for that!

⚅ ⚁ Love remains: but this is where the romance stops and the marriage begins!

⚅ ⚃ He likes you, and why not?

⚅ ⚃ Your progress is at a snail's pace at the moment.

⚅ ⚄ She finds poor men unattractive. Does that answer your question?

⚅ ⚅ Yes, he does — and he always will!

The Oracle
Page 7

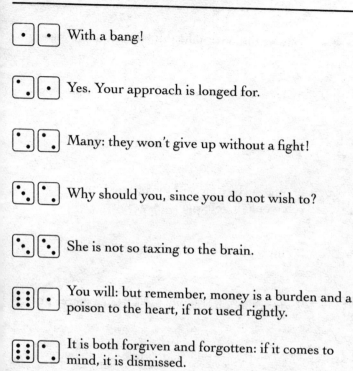

With a bang!

Yes. Your approach is longed for.

Many: they won't give up without a fight!

Why should you, since you do not wish to?

She is not so taxing to the brain.

You will: but remember, money is a burden and a poison to the heart, if not used rightly.

It is both forgiven and forgotten: if it comes to mind, it is dismissed.

I see a little boat on a river: If this is your destination, you will soon move: if it is your view from your present window, you stay put.

Do not travel by water at present.

Apologise for your stupidity!

She loves you — and you alone.

The Oracle
Page 8

⚁ ⚀ (1-1)	Oh, you little wretch! Put him out of his misery!
⚁ ⚀ (2-1)	As favourable as possible, in the circumstances.
⚁ ⚁ (2-2)	A warning should be issued, no more.
⚂ ⚂ (3-3)	On the surface, accept the promise; but behave as you would if you knew it was false.
⚃ ⚃ (4-4)	If you avoid debauchery, you will.
⚅ ⚀ (6-1)	Widow, though you will have been a merry one!
⚅ ⚁ (6-2)	That anything you can do, they can do better!
⚅ ⚂ (6-3)	How can you, when you change direction so often?
⚅ ⚃ (6-4)	Thirteen — and the last shall cure you of the first.
⚅ ⚄ (6-5)	It is becoming less likely.
⚅ ⚅ (6-6)	Love conquers all! You can marry him if you will, and have a long and happy marriage together.

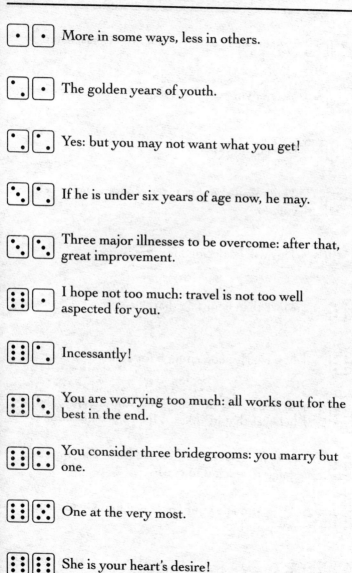

More in some ways, less in others.

The golden years of youth.

Yes: but you may not want what you get!

If he is under six years of age now, he may.

Three major illnesses to be overcome: after that, great improvement.

I hope not too much: travel is not too well aspected for you.

Incessantly!

You are worrying too much: all works out for the best in the end.

You consider three bridegrooms: you marry but one.

One at the very most.

She is your heart's desire!

The Oracle
Page 10

⚀⚀ Two omens, contrary: win now — lose later.

⚁⚀ Yes, moving of job or home.

⚁⚁ Consult an expert.

⚂⚁ Think well about it, three separate times, before you do.

⚂⚂ This will be decided for you.

⚃⚀ More than your fair share.

⚃⚁ Not nearly soon enough for you.

⚃⚂ In this home, the wife rules, and the husband believes that he does. A happy state of affairs.

⚃⚃ She thinks you have a lot to learn, and that she is going to teach it to you!

⚅⚅ Many outside your circle will know your name, if not your face.

⚅⚅ You are a delightful spectacle!

The Oracle
Page 11

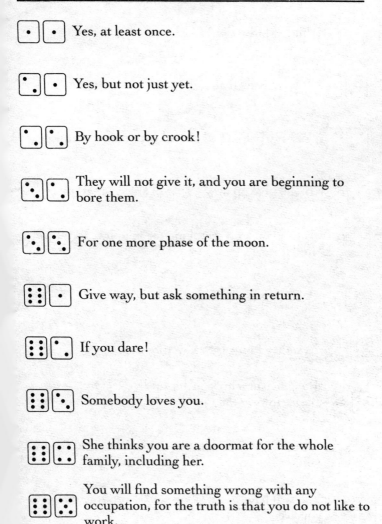

Yes, at least once.

Yes, but not just yet.

By hook or by crook!

They will not give it, and you are beginning to bore them.

For one more phase of the moon.

Give way, but ask something in return.

If you dare!

Somebody loves you.

She thinks you are a doormat for the whole family, including her.

You will find something wrong with any occupation, for the truth is that you do not like to work.

Yes — apart from that nose!

The Oracle

⚀⚀ Filthy, filthy rich!

⚁⚀ It is suspected already.

⚁⚁ Yes, my pet — and so will your sense of guilt!

⚂⚁ If you give up now, you will always regret it.

⚂⚂ When you stop searching for happiness, you will find it easily.

⚅⚀ At first, nothing. Later, revenge.

⚅⚁ Yes, they know they can trust you.

⚅⚂ Romance in marriage *can* survive children — please inform the Oracle if you discover how it is done.

⚅⚃ He thinks you 'a typical woman' and is baffled by you.

⚅⚄ You will have a very long wait if you stay where you are.

⚅⚅ I hope not, for her sake, poor lady. It would be difficult to prise it out of your paws!

The Oracle
Page 13

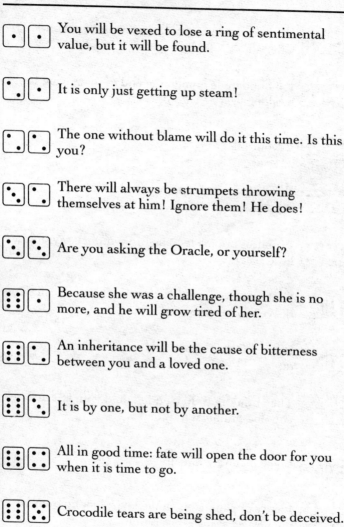

You will be vexed to lose a ring of sentimental value, but it will be found.

It is only just getting up steam!

The one without blame will do it this time. Is this you?

There will always be strumpets throwing themselves at him! Ignore them! He does!

Are you asking the Oracle, or yourself?

Because she was a challenge, though she is no more, and he will grow tired of her.

An inheritance will be the cause of bitterness between you and a loved one.

It is by one, but not by another.

All in good time: fate will open the door for you when it is time to go.

Crocodile tears are being shed, don't be deceived.

Now that, as they say, is the question! And only you know the answer to it.

The Oracle

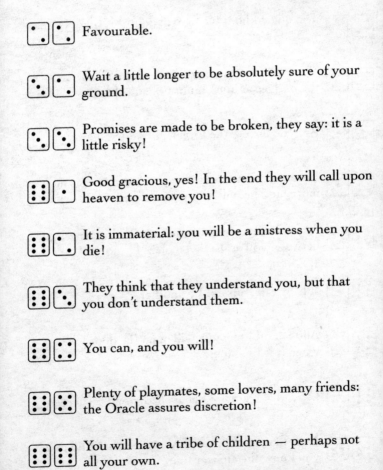

With a grey head on the pillow next to yours. Cherish old age!

Do not dangle him on the end of that string for too long, lest he let go!

Favourable.

Wait a little longer to be absolutely sure of your ground.

Promises are made to be broken, they say: it is a little risky!

Good gracious, yes! In the end they will call upon heaven to remove you!

It is immaterial: you will be a mistress when you die!

They think that they understand you, but that you don't understand them.

You can, and you will!

Plenty of playmates, some lovers, many friends: the Oracle assures discretion!

You will have a tribe of children — perhaps not all your own.

The Oracle

That there is more to you than meets the eye!

He loves you to madness!

Your forties, and late sixties.

No. It is not for you.

No! He likes himself well enough as he is!

You are often ailing, but rarely ill — you are the original swinging gate that never breaks.

I think you have done the bulk of your travelling already.

No, but they think of you.

It is not for long, but seems an eternity to you.

One, with whom you will find great content.

Yes, but it will be a surprise package.

The Oracle

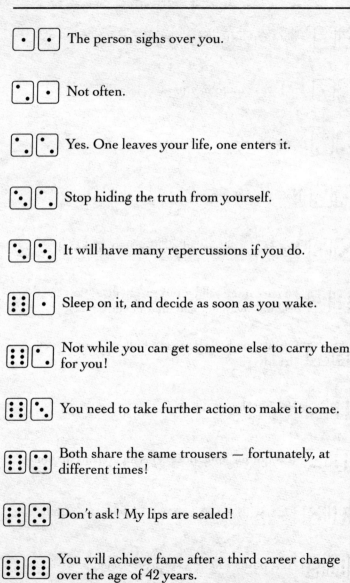

The person sighs over you.

Not often.

Yes. One leaves your life, one enters it.

Stop hiding the truth from yourself.

It will have many repercussions if you do.

Sleep on it, and decide as soon as you wake.

Not while you can get someone else to carry them for you!

You need to take further action to make it come.

Both share the same trousers — fortunately, at different times!

Don't ask! My lips are sealed!

You will achieve fame after a third career change over the age of 42 years.

The Oracle
Page 17

How could they forget?

You will live and work in two continents, and perhaps three.

If you hurry; time flies!

By using up one of your nine lives.

You know the explanation already: your object is to humiliate, you pecking jackdaw!

All that is necessary to put it to flight is a little cherishing. Turn to a kind friend.

Decide what you want and give *them* an ultimatum.

Yes, you have a good chance of success.

What was lost will be found.

She likes you; and her affection continues to grow.

If your occupation is that of lying on a silken couch, eating bon-bons, then yes. Otherwise, no.

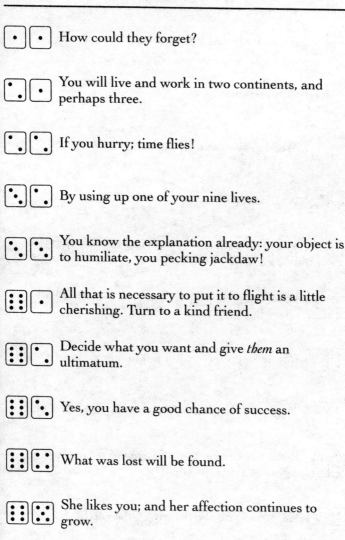

The Oracle

⚀⚀ If you wait long enough, yes.

⚁⚀ Comfortable.

⚁⚁ Tread very carefully, especially now.

⚂⚁ No, scatterbrain!

⚂⚂ You are wasting precious time and energy: you cannot win.

⚅⚀ Love brings happiness back, as though it had never been absent.

⚅⚁ It is an open secret, known to many.

⚅⚂ They don't get much of a chance, now do they?

⚅⚃ Romance can revive: this usually occurs just before the next pregnancy.

⚅⚄ He thinks you are the salt of the earth.

⚅⚅ You make two strides forward in the next twelve months: one at midsummer, one at Christmas.

The Oracle
Page 19

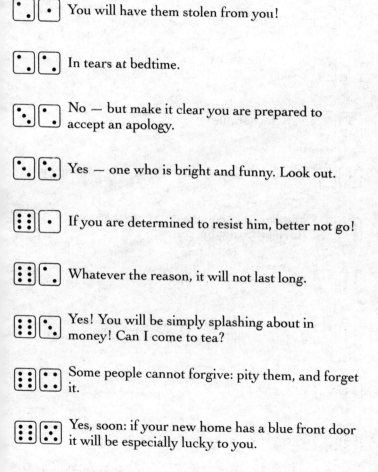

Only if you ask a fairy!

You will have them stolen from you!

In tears at bedtime.

No — but make it clear you are prepared to accept an apology.

Yes — one who is bright and funny. Look out.

If you are determined to resist him, better not go!

Whatever the reason, it will not last long.

Yes! You will be simply splashing about in money! Can I come to tea?

Some people cannot forgive: pity them, and forget it.

Yes, soon: if your new home has a blue front door it will be especially lucky to you.

Your pride brings a fall.

The Oracle
Page 20

He is kissing the mirror, and thinking himself a fine fellow.

Calm after storms: yes, you will be happy.

Just remember that as you make him suffer now, so you will suffer in the future!

Very favourable.

Yes, if you are prepared to face the consequences.

You have a trusting nature: how can you help it? But a little caution, please.

A long life, and a happy one.

You will have been spinster, wife, divorcee, widow — and some of them more than once!

That you are a good friend to them.

If you cultivate tunnel vision, yes. Distractions are your bugbear.

Well, dear, either you have a very loving heart, or an incurably romantic nature: we are past two dozen, and still counting!

The Oracle
Page 21

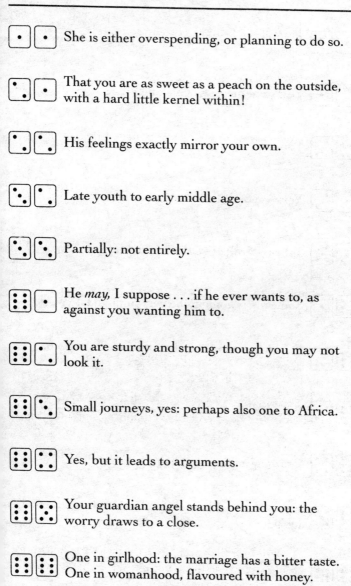

She is either overspending, or planning to do so.

That you are as sweet as a peach on the outside, with a hard little kernel within!

His feelings exactly mirror your own.

Late youth to early middle age.

Partially: not entirely.

He *may*, I suppose . . . if he ever wants to, as against you wanting him to.

You are sturdy and strong, though you may not look it.

Small journeys, yes: perhaps also one to Africa.

Yes, but it leads to arguments.

Your guardian angel stands behind you: the worry draws to a close.

One in girlhood: the marriage has a bitter taste. One in womanhood, flavoured with honey.

The Oracle
Page 22

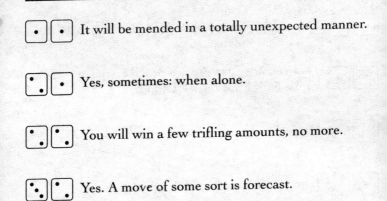

⚀⚀ It will be mended in a totally unexpected manner.

⚁⚀ Yes, sometimes: when alone.

⚁⚁ You will win a few trifling amounts, no more.

⚂⚂ Yes. A move of some sort is forecast.

⚂⚂ Take control: seize the initiative.

⚃⚀ Someone is going to be very annoyed if you do!

⚃⚁ Decide to whom or what you owe loyalty, then decide.

⚃⚂ Yes, always.

⚃⚃ It is winging its way to you.

⚃⚄ The husband is king: his wife, queen: all else their subjects.

⚃⚅ She likes you, and is growing to love you very dearly.

The Oracle

Remember the old saying — a lie is like a mouse-dropping in clear soup. Very visible — especially the way *you* tell them.

They will, I promise!

The Oracle sees mountains, the time one to three years.

Yes, yes, yes!

You will walk away from it through a door opened by a loved one.

Do not press for it: in time, it may be given.

It will last for as long as you cling to the past.

Change the subject whenever it arises.

It will cost you a few tears if you do.

Pennies from heaven fall on you.

She thinks your ideas of family bear a marked resemblance to the Mafia.

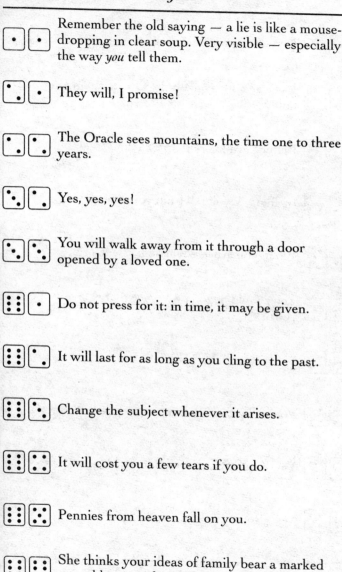

The Oracle
Page 24

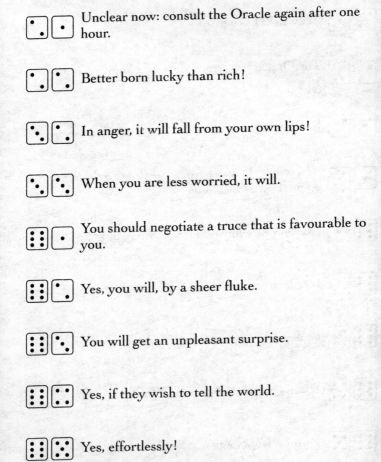

Choose the one that makes you laugh.

Unclear now: consult the Oracle again after one hour.

Better born lucky than rich!

In anger, it will fall from your own lips!

When you are less worried, it will.

You should negotiate a truce that is favourable to you.

Yes, you will, by a sheer fluke.

You will get an unpleasant surprise.

Yes, if they wish to tell the world.

Yes, effortlessly!

He likes you no better than his own mother — and thinks little enough of her.

The Oracle
Page 25

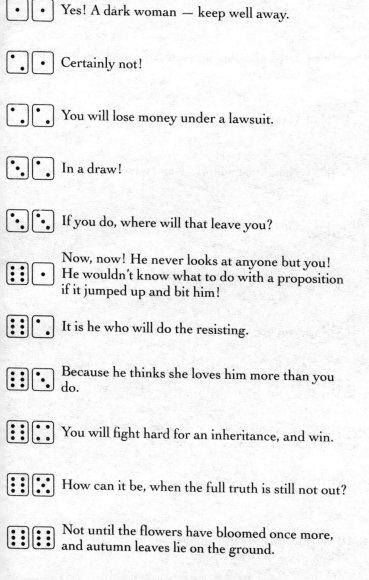

Yes! A dark woman — keep well away.

Certainly not!

You will lose money under a lawsuit.

In a draw!

If you do, where will that leave you?

Now, now! He never looks at anyone but you! He wouldn't know what to do with a proposition if it jumped up and bit him!

It is he who will do the resisting.

Because he thinks she loves him more than you do.

You will fight hard for an inheritance, and win.

How can it be, when the full truth is still not out?

Not until the flowers have bloomed once more, and autumn leaves lie on the ground.

The Oracle
Page 26

⚀⚀ Oh, I hope you will not!

⚁⚀ He is grinding his teeth, and thinking himself hard done by.

⚂⚂ Happy, healthy, wealthy, and wise!

⚃⚂ Naughty, naughty! Kiss and make up!

⚃⚃ Fair, no more.

⚅⚀ Yes, if your status allows it.

⚅⚁ Not for a *moment!*

⚅⚃ It is as you decree: premature death is brought on by dissipation and excess. Take heed!

⚅⚄ You will be a wife — but it is not only your husband who will mourn.

⚅⚄ That you are at your best under adversity.

⚅⚅ With help from many hands, you will.

The Oracle
Page 27

What is lost shall yet be found.

She is frowning at your photograph.

That you are a rough diamond, with a heart of gold.

Differently.

Your fifties — and on looking back, your childhood.

Yes, by endeavour.

How many tender creatures have asked this question before? And received the answer: *never!*

Bored equals ill for you: you droop and succumb without occupation. Do something, or catch something!

Mainly in Europe.

Only to rant and rave!

Be patient a little longer, and your problem will solve itself.

The Oracle

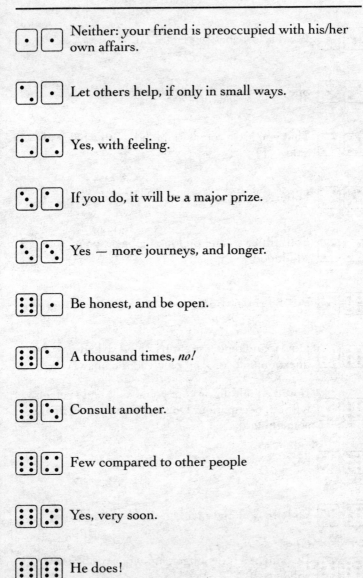

Neither: your friend is preoccupied with his/her own affairs.

Let others help, if only in small ways.

Yes, with feeling.

If you do, it will be a major prize.

Yes — more journeys, and longer.

Be honest, and be open.

A thousand times, *no!*

Consult another.

Few compared to other people

Yes, very soon.

He does!

The Oracle

⚀⚀ Alas, too late.

⚁⚁ That would be beneath you, little angel. Besides, the truth is already known.

⚂⚂ They certainly have good cause to.

⚃⚃ You will be based in America, and Europe.

⚄⚄ You will be a star, as you have always known you would!

⚅⚀ By staying cool, and keeping your head.

⚅⚁ If they give you an explanation, you will give them a sermon. This is why they do not wish to do it.

⚅⚂ Something will happen in the next few weeks to wipe it out of your mind.

⚅⚃ Use a little subtlety and guile!

⚅⚄ So long as it can be undone if necessary, yes.

⚅⚅ I bring you a kiss from an absent friend.

The Oracle
Page 30

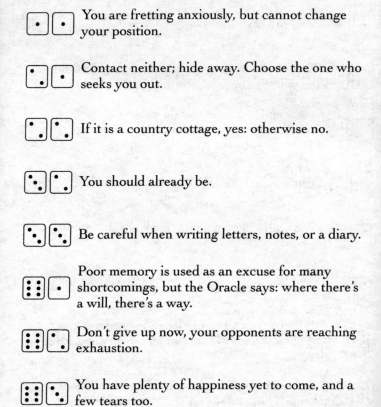

You are fretting anxiously, but cannot change your position.

Contact neither; hide away. Choose the one who seeks you out.

If it is a country cottage, yes: otherwise no.

You should already be.

Be careful when writing letters, notes, or a diary.

Poor memory is used as an excuse for many shortcomings, but the Oracle says: where there's a will, there's a way.

Don't give up now, your opponents are reaching exhaustion.

You have plenty of happiness yet to come, and a few tears too.

You will be deceived in turn.

No, you nosey parker — they do not!

Not after the first 21 years, no.

The Oracle
Page 31

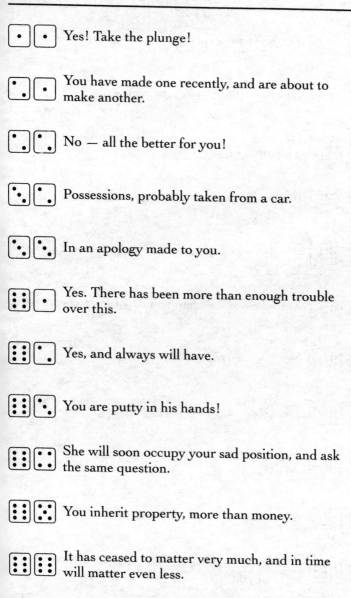

Yes! Take the plunge!

You have made one recently, and are about to make another.

No — all the better for you!

Possessions, probably taken from a car.

In an apology made to you.

Yes. There has been more than enough trouble over this.

Yes, and always will have.

You are putty in his hands!

She will soon occupy your sad position, and ask the same question.

You inherit property, more than money.

It has ceased to matter very much, and in time will matter even less.

The Oracle
Page 32

[⚀][⚀]	The one least expected to.
[⚁][⚀]	One day, at the right time, you will.
[⚁][⚁]	He is taking his own pulse, and wishing a fair white hand was taking it for him.
[⚂][⚁]	If it is not, you will only have yourself to blame.
[⚂][⚂]	Oh, just a *little* longer won't hurt, will it?
[⚅][⚀]	More favourable than you may have expected.
[⚅][⚁]	No. Your suspicions are groundless.
[⚅][⚂]	The Oracle says no, but you will say yes.
[⚅][⚃]	Physical laziness is your enemy, and could shorten your life.
[⚅][⚄]	A wealthy widow, and a kind one.
[⚅][⚅]	You drive them mad — but they cannot manage without you!

The Oracle
Page 33

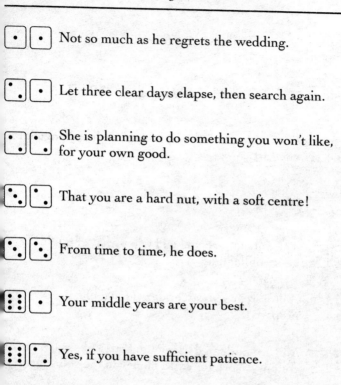	Not so much as he regrets the wedding.
	Let three clear days elapse, then search again.
	She is planning to do something you won't like, for your own good.
	That you are a hard nut, with a soft centre!
	From time to time, he does.
	Your middle years are your best.
	Yes, if you have sufficient patience.
	Put it to the test: if he promises that he will, say nothing, and observe. It may happen.
	Yes — but don't neglect a weight problem. It could lead to other things.
	You are going a long distance overland, perhaps in America.
	They do not think of you, so they do not speak of you.

The Oracle
Page 34

Yes, and will regret it more.

Your friend is troubled by many difficulties.

Cry on the shoulder of someone who is longing to comfort you.

Almost never, now.

The only lottery you will win is that of finding your soulmate!

A crossroads in career or personal life: be prepared.

You are under a dark cloud: better times are coming. Work for extra money in the short term.

Only if you are proud of yourself for what you wish to confess.

You know in your heart what it is.

No. Those who love you, help you.

You will have some news before long, then a wait, then the rest of the message will come.

The Oracle
Page 35

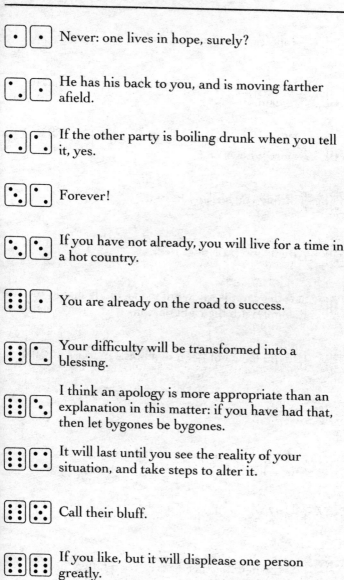

⚀ ⚀   Never: one lives in hope, surely?

⚁ ⚁   He has his back to you, and is moving farther afield.

⚂ ⚂   If the other party is boiling drunk when you tell it, yes.

⚃ ⚃   Forever!

⚄ ⚄   If you have not already, you will live for a time in a hot country.

⚅ ⚀   You are already on the road to success.

⚅ ⚁   Your difficulty will be transformed into a blessing.

⚅ ⚂   I think an apology is more appropriate than an explanation in this matter: if you have had that, then let bygones be bygones.

⚅ ⚃   It will last until you see the reality of your situation, and take steps to alter it.

⚅ ⚄   Call their bluff.

⚅ ⚅   If you like, but it will displease one person greatly.

The Oracle
Page 36

⚁ (1-1)	Talk less, and smile more.
(2-1)	It is not a happy situation, but you are fated to remain together.
(2-2)	Choose the one who smells the fresher, and is the more wholesome.
(3-1)	Surely you already have it?
(3-3)	Rich, and possibly titled.
(6-1)	Your secret is safe with me — but it should be shared with the right person.
(6-2)	If you have not left it in a bottle or glass, it will!
(6-3)	Save your strength: it is hopeless.
(6-4)	Happiness will return to light up your life. It is most likely to be found close to home.
(6-5)	They will gain the upper hand — and that would never do.
(6-6)	Yes, when they need a true friend, they do.

The Oracle
Page 37

⚀ ⚀ A charming rogue.

⚁ ⚀ If you do, it must be completely.

⚁ ⚁ One bears a grudge, still green and fresh, from long ago.

⚂ ⚂ You know it will!

⚂ ⚂ No, other than trifling things.

⚃ ⚀ It will be left aside for another day.

⚃ ⚂ Yes: you will shame them by so doing.

⚃ ⚂ You have had, but not now.

⚃ ⚄ In broad daylight, in a crowded street: perhaps. But I wouldn't put money on it!

⚃ ⚄ Because he is suffering from temporary insanity, that's why!

⚃ ⚄ Have a care, child. The Oracle scents avarice: be careful you are not cut out of the will for spite!

The Oracle
Page 38

⚁ ⚁ Like a pig that's got hold of a lipstick.

⚁ ⚁ This battle should be stopped: both will be severely hurt.

⚁ ⚁ Not unless you ferret it out, and that would be most unwise.

⚂ ⚁ He is paying compliments to another woman.

⚃ ⚃ Happily enough — but not quite as happy as your middle years.

⚅ ⚀ Forgive him now, while he still repents!

⚅ ⚀ It will be the best that can be managed at the time.

⚅ ⚂ Perhaps later — not now.

⚅ ⚃ If the promise is made in front of a large congregation, in church, in a ceremony which places a ring on your finger: yes. If not, no.

⚅ ⚄ A century of years: in the end, death will come in as a welcome visitor.

⚅ ⚅ A widow, who could have remarried again and again if she pleased.

The Oracle

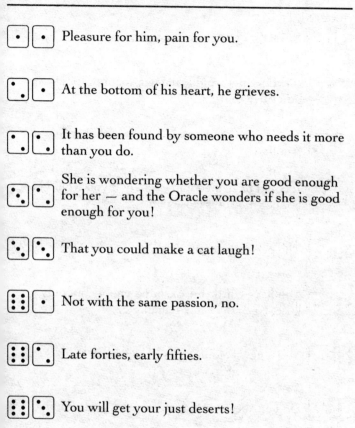

Pleasure for him, pain for you.

At the bottom of his heart, he grieves.

It has been found by someone who needs it more than you do.

She is wondering whether you are good enough for her — and the Oracle wonders if she is good enough for you!

That you could make a cat laugh!

Not with the same passion, no.

Late forties, early fifties.

You will get your just deserts!

The Oracle will not deign to answer this question, on the grounds that it would be stating the obvious.

Good enough for you to get into a great deal of mischief in your life!

Mostly, for long journeys, in the next five years: after that circumstances will keep your travels short.

The Oracle
Page 40

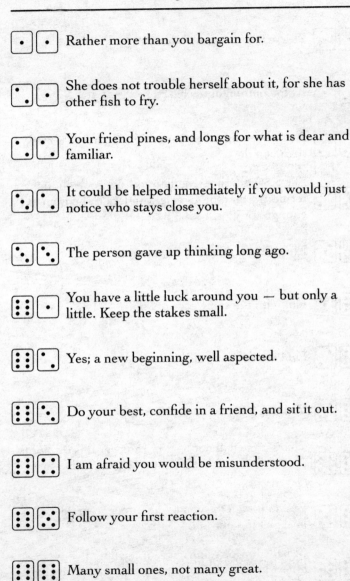

⚁ ⚀	Rather more than you bargain for.
⚁ ⚀	She does not trouble herself about it, for she has other fish to fry.
⚁ ⚁	Your friend pines, and longs for what is dear and familiar.
⚂ ⚀	It could be helped immediately if you would just notice who stays close you.
⚂ ⚂	The person gave up thinking long ago.
⚃ ⚀	You have a little luck around you — but only a little. Keep the stakes small.
⚃ ⚁	Yes; a new beginning, well aspected.
⚃ ⚂	Do your best, confide in a friend, and sit it out.
⚃ ⚃	I am afraid you would be misunderstood.
⚃ ⚄	Follow your first reaction.
⚃ ⚃	Many small ones, not many great.

The Oracle
Page 41

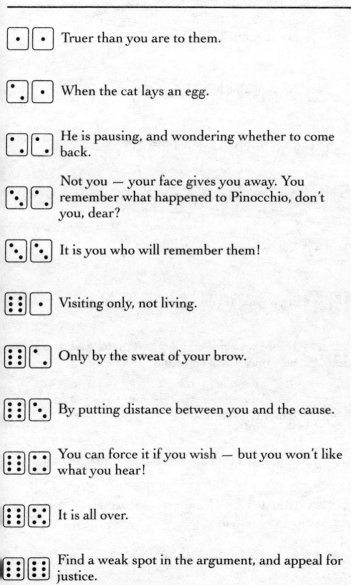

⚀ ⚀   Truer than you are to them.

⚁ ⚀   When the cat lays an egg.

⚁ ⚁   He is pausing, and wondering whether to come back.

⚂ ⚂   Not you — your face gives you away. You remember what happened to Pinocchio, don't you, dear?

⚂ ⚂   It is you who will remember them!

⚅ ⚀   Visiting only, not living.

⚅ ⚁   Only by the sweat of your brow.

⚅ ⚂   By putting distance between you and the cause.

⚅ ⚅   You can force it if you wish — but you won't like what you hear!

⚅ ⚄   It is all over.

⚅ ⚅   Find a weak spot in the argument, and appeal for justice.

The Oracle
Page 42

⚀ ⚀ For the time being, yes.

⚁ ⚀ Nothing: his heart is given to another.

⚁ ⚁ No, you would be happier apart.

⚂ ⚂ Ask me again when one of them has chosen you!

⚃ ⚃ Yes, when you least expect it.

⚅ ⚀ If you are not now, you never will be.

⚅ ⚁ If it be an old secret, leave it in the past. If it be a new one, it will come out in the end.

⚅ ⚂ No. Give up the struggle, and have pens and paper in every room!

⚅ ⚃ Yes, just a little longer: but set a time limit now.

⚅ ⚄ You will have happiness and sadness in your life, as will we all!

⚅ ⚅ You will be treated with kindness that increases your guilt.

The Oracle
Page 43

Yes, she glows with love for you, like a little glow-worm.

Older than you, and flatulent.

If in career — no, not now.

You have made a number of enemies, but they are all helpless in the face of your goodness.

Be careful what you wish, for dreams come true!

You will lose money through carelessness.

In hurt pride.

No. It would precipitate an avalanche.

You have one who is everything that you are not.

That strange sound you hear is the Oracle, laughing.

He shows this preference to pay you out.

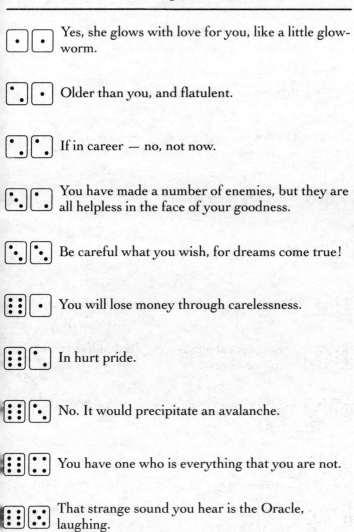

The Oracle
Page 44

⚁⚁ Yes, if you wish to be maid, cook and bottlewasher, serving a lord!

⚂⚀ Pretty, small, and iron-willed.

⚂⚂ The weaker of the two, by use of tears in the face of strength.

⚃⚃ You know quite enough.

⚄⚄ He is scowling, and counting up his money.

⚅⚀ Settle for what you can, then you will.

⚅⚂ Don't play cat and mouse, dear, unless you wish to live on cheese!

⚅⚄ More favourable to them.

⚅⚃ Not yet.

⚅⚄ For what it's worth, yes: keep your wits sharp behind your smile!

⚅⚅ The star guiding you from birth continues to do so until the 93rd year of your life.

The Oracle
Page 45

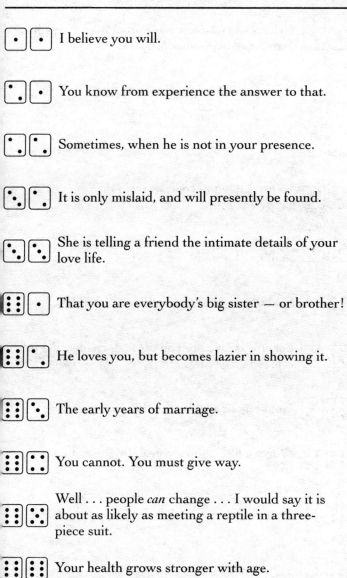

I believe you will.

You know from experience the answer to that.

Sometimes, when he is not in your presence.

It is only mislaid, and will presently be found.

She is telling a friend the intimate details of your love life.

That you are everybody's big sister — or brother!

He loves you, but becomes lazier in showing it.

The early years of marriage.

You cannot. You must give way.

Well . . . people *can* change . . . I would say it is about as likely as meeting a reptile in a three-piece suit.

Your health grows stronger with age.

The Oracle

⚀⚀ Well, you certainly have your moments, I will draw a veil over when they are!

⚁⚀ She'll eat you for breakfast!

⚁⚁ Sometimes, when she has need of you.

⚂⚂ Your friend lives completely in the present, and is happy enough.

⚃⚃ With tears to wash away the pain, and the comfort of friends.

⚅⚀ It would surprise you to know how often.

⚅⚁ Fortune is given to you through chance: the price is making enemies.

⚅⚃ Not without a lot more effort on your part.

⚅⚁ Worry a little more, instead of pretending to do so.

⚅⚄ That would be foolish indeed.

⚅⚅ Opt for the new.

The Oracle

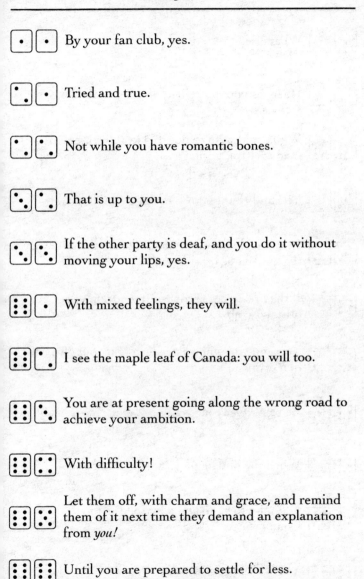

By your fan club, yes.

Tried and true.

Not while you have romantic bones.

That is up to you.

If the other party is deaf, and you do it without moving your lips, yes.

With mixed feelings, they will.

I see the maple leaf of Canada: you will too.

You are at present going along the wrong road to achieve your ambition.

With difficulty!

Let them off, with charm and grace, and remind them of it next time they demand an explanation from *you!*

Until you are prepared to settle for less.

The Oracle

⚀⚀ What else?

⚁⚀ He loves you more than he ever intended to.

⚂⚀ Who could wish to do so? He will trifle with you, then cast you adrift.

⚃⚀ Yes, and count your blessings.

⚄⚄ Leave aside the cleverest, and take the one with the kindest heart.

⚅⚀ If the dream concerns your children, yes: otherwise no.

⚅⚁ Yes, and you will waste some of it, and give a lot of it away.

⚅⚃ Be calm. Deny it.

⚅⚂ When the budgie plays a trumpet, it will!

⚅⚄ Yes, a lot to gain: and a lot to lose, too. Compromise.

⚅⚅ You will, I promise you!

The Oracle
Page 49

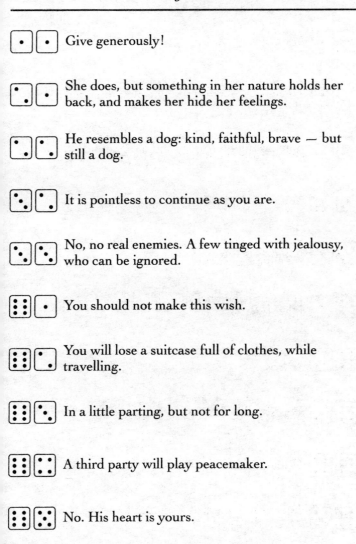

Give generously!

She does, but something in her nature holds her back, and makes her hide her feelings.

He resembles a dog: kind, faithful, brave — but still a dog.

It is pointless to continue as you are.

No, no real enemies. A few tinged with jealousy, who can be ignored.

You should not make this wish.

You will lose a suitcase full of clothes, while travelling.

In a little parting, but not for long.

A third party will play peacemaker.

No. His heart is yours.

Yes, with ease. He will look so horrid!

The Oracle
Page 50

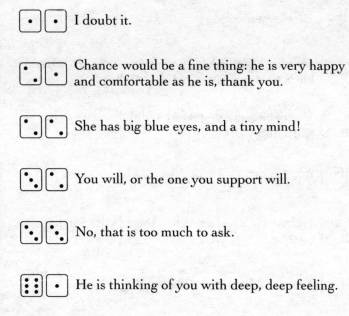

▣ ▣ I doubt it.

▣ ▣ Chance would be a fine thing: he is very happy and comfortable as he is, thank you.

▣ ▣ She has big blue eyes, and a tiny mind!

▣ ▣ You will, or the one you support will.

▣ ▣ No, that is too much to ask.

▣ ▣ He is thinking of you with deep, deep feeling.

▣ ▣ If one important change takes place between now and then — yes.

▣ ▣ Forgive, but don't quite forget.

▣ ▣ Unfavourable.

▣ ▣ Yes — out with it!

▣ ▣ If you trust the maker of it, yes.

The Oracle

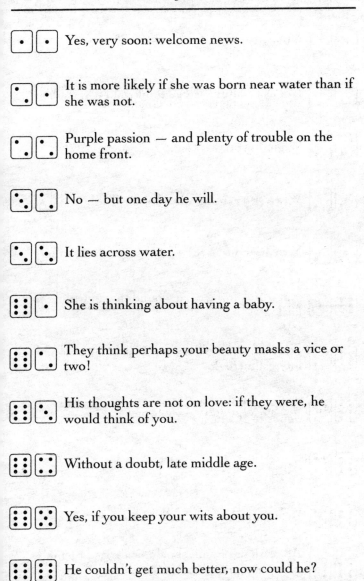

Yes, very soon: welcome news.

It is more likely if she was born near water than if she was not.

Purple passion — and plenty of trouble on the home front.

No — but one day he will.

It lies across water.

She is thinking about having a baby.

They think perhaps your beauty masks a vice or two!

His thoughts are not on love: if they were, he would think of you.

Without a doubt, late middle age.

Yes, if you keep your wits about you.

He couldn't get much better, now could he?

The Oracle
Page 52

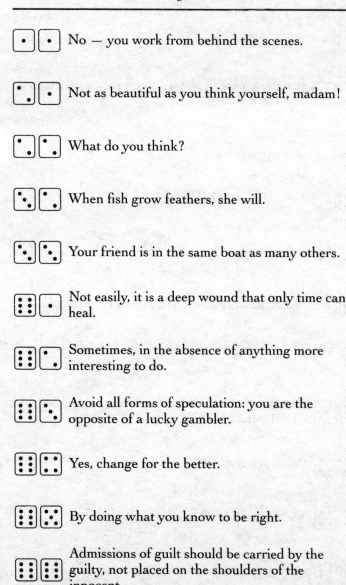

No — you work from behind the scenes.

Not as beautiful as you think yourself, madam!

What do you think?

When fish grow feathers, she will.

Your friend is in the same boat as many others.

Not easily, it is a deep wound that only time can heal.

Sometimes, in the absence of anything more interesting to do.

Avoid all forms of speculation: you are the opposite of a lucky gambler.

Yes, change for the better.

By doing what you know to be right.

Admissions of guilt should be carried by the guilty, not placed on the shoulders of the innocent.

The Oracle
Page 53

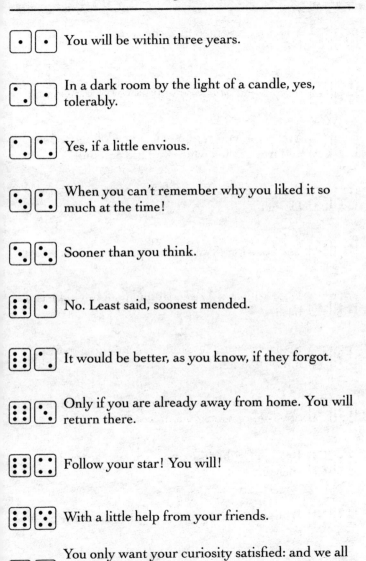

You will be within three years.

In a dark room by the light of a candle, yes, tolerably.

Yes, if a little envious.

When you can't remember why you liked it so much at the time!

Sooner than you think.

No. Least said, soonest mended.

It would be better, as you know, if they forgot.

Only if you are already away from home. You will return there.

Follow your star! You will!

With a little help from your friends.

You only want your curiosity satisfied: and we all know what curiosity did to that poor old puss-cat, don't we?

The Oracle
Page 54

You are prevented by circumstances. Be patient a little longer.

Well — not *only* for your money!

Yes, when you are bowing and scraping to him — and truth to tell, when you are not, too!

Praise him, and agree with him when he praises himself.

Someone bars your exit — perhaps it is yourself.

Why ask me, when you fully intend to hold on to both?

Never give up hope: nothing is truly impossible.

Yes — beyond the dreams of avarice, or indeed, of you!

Remember that the price of a kept secret is silence.

Some memories are evergreen. Forget the others!

Cease fire — but drive a hard bargain.

The Oracle
Page 55

⚀⚀ Start nothing new until after new moon.

⚁⚀ Stop trying so hard.

⚁⚁ She does, she does!

⚂⚀ Like a bear with a sore head!

⚂⚂ If you do, there will be no turning the clock back.

⚅⚀ No. Feelings do not run strong enough for that.

⚅⚁ Yes — and the other one you are not mentioning will, too!

⚅⚂ You will lose money in cash, on more than one occasion: kind friends help out in the disaster.

⚅⚃ In a better understanding.

⚅⚄ Not this time.

⚅⚅ It would be a foolish young lady who so wasted her time!

The Oracle
Page 56

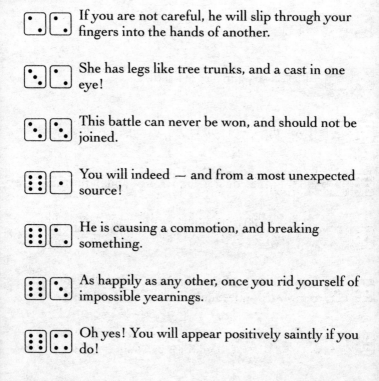

⚀⚀ Enough to outrage the community!

⚁⚀ Two little angels, just like you!

⚂⚀ If you are not careful, he will slip through your fingers into the hands of another.

⚃⚀ She has legs like tree trunks, and a cast in one eye!

⚄⚀ This battle can never be won, and should not be joined.

⚅⚀ You will indeed — and from a most unexpected source!

⚅⚁ He is causing a commotion, and breaking something.

⚅⚂ As happily as any other, once you rid yourself of impossible yearnings.

⚅⚃ Oh yes! You will appear positively saintly if you do!

⚅⚄ An equal compromise.

⚅⚅ Not without very good reason.

The Oracle
Page 57

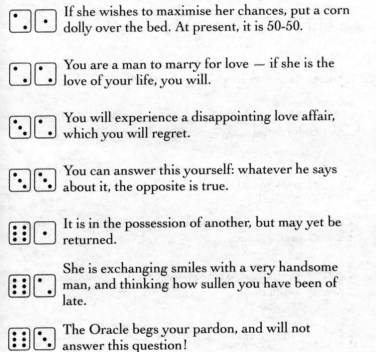

Two: one for love, one for money.

If she wishes to maximise her chances, put a corn dolly over the bed. At present, it is 50-50.

You are a man to marry for love — if she is the love of your life, you will.

You will experience a disappointing love affair, which you will regret.

You can answer this yourself: whatever he says about it, the opposite is true.

It is in the possession of another, but may yet be returned.

She is exchanging smiles with a very handsome man, and thinking how sullen you have been of late.

The Oracle begs your pardon, and will not answer this question!

He loves you, and takes you for granted, where once he treasured your every glance.

From thirty-five years onwards, reaching a peak in old age.

No. It is a lost cause.

The Oracle
Page 58

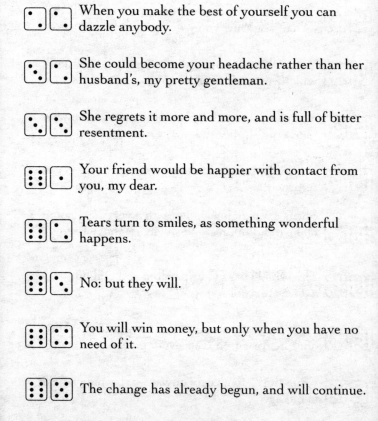

That you are a pearl!

Not exactly famous, but you make a mark wherever you go. Everyone remembers you!

When you make the best of yourself you can dazzle anybody.

She could become your headache rather than her husband's, my pretty gentleman.

She regrets it more and more, and is full of bitter resentment.

Your friend would be happier with contact from you, my dear.

Tears turn to smiles, as something wonderful happens.

No: but they will.

You will win money, but only when you have no need of it.

The change has already begun, and will continue.

Work and economise now: in a year your prospects are transformed!

The Oracle
Page 59

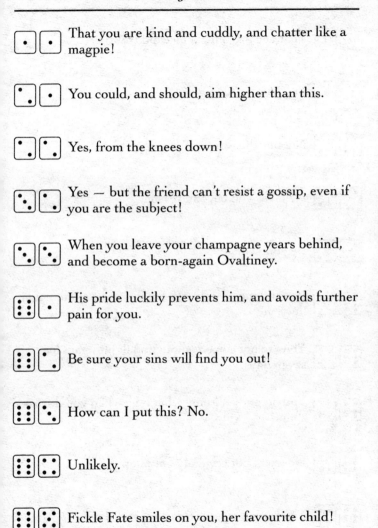	That you are kind and cuddly, and chatter like a magpie!
	You could, and should, aim higher than this.
	Yes, from the knees down!
	Yes — but the friend can't resist a gossip, even if you are the subject!
	When you leave your champagne years behind, and become a born-again Ovaltiney.
	His pride luckily prevents him, and avoids further pain for you.
	Be sure your sins will find you out!
	How can I put this? No.
	Unlikely.
	Fickle Fate smiles on you, her favourite child!
	Resign yourself. This is one difficulty that cannot be dodged.

The Oracle
Page 60

That you are quite a nice old trout!

Yes. You are doing very well.

No, but she wants your money too.

He loves you beyond reason.

Be yourself.

If you think of yourself, no; if you attend to your duty, yes.

You are not sincere enough. Ask me again in seven days.

You do not yet know what it is: when you do, ask again!

Not rich, but certainly not poor.

Your secret is your treasure: guard it well!

There now! You cannot remember your question, can you?

The Oracle
Page 61

After a whirl of activity, you will.

Beware of false friends.

Make her laugh — and *listen* to her.

She did once, but the tie loosens, for lack of affection.

Full of conceit, with nothing to be conceited about.

Yes. Something definitely needs to change in your life.

Yes — one you think a friend is pouring poison into a foolish but beloved ear.

This wish must be asked of the next garden gnome you find, sitting on his mushroom. If he nods, it will come true.

Something will be taken by stealth.

With tears, and kisses.

A look and a smile will be enough to make a start.

The Oracle
Page 62

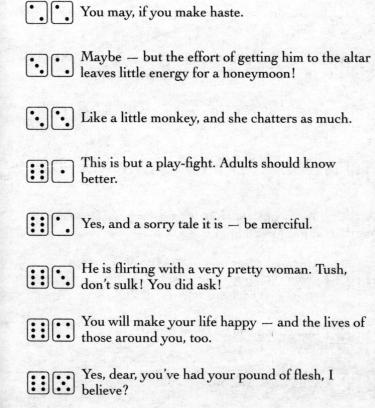

Yes, my pet — and more than one!

Too many!

You may, if you make haste.

Maybe — but the effort of getting him to the altar leaves little energy for a honeymoon!

Like a little monkey, and she chatters as much.

This is but a play-fight. Adults should know better.

Yes, and a sorry tale it is — be merciful.

He is flirting with a very pretty woman. Tush, don't sulk! You did ask!

You will make your life happy — and the lives of those around you, too.

Yes, dear, you've had your pound of flesh, I believe?

More favourable than it at first appears.

The Oracle
Page 63

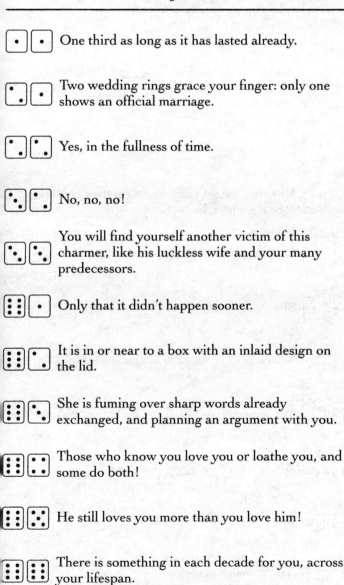

One third as long as it has lasted already.

Two wedding rings grace your finger: only one shows an official marriage.

Yes, in the fullness of time.

No, no, no!

You will find yourself another victim of this charmer, like his luckless wife and your many predecessors.

Only that it didn't happen sooner.

It is in or near to a box with an inlaid design on the lid.

She is fuming over sharp words already exchanged, and planning an argument with you.

Those who know you love you or loathe you, and some do both!

He still loves you more than you love him!

There is something in each decade for you, across your lifespan.

The Oracle
Page 64

Oh! I think we both know the answer to that!

She has not quite made up her mind about you, yet.

Famous for *something*, certainly!

You are thought more beautiful than you are, such is your style.

Fun, excitement, and a rather high price tag.

She says no. The Oracle says yes.

Your friend is not very happy at present.

You cannot hurry healing. Be brave, my dear.

Are not their thoughts their own?

No, not even if you try from morning till night.

Yes. A major one.

The Oracle
Page 65

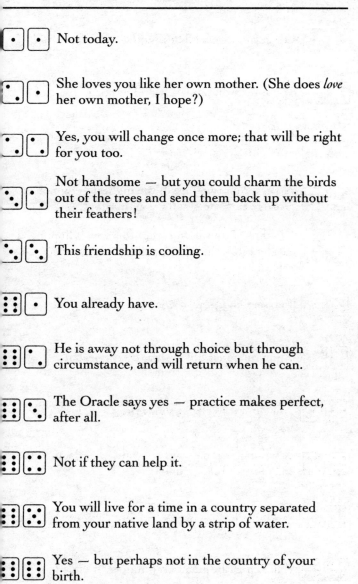

Not today.

She loves you like her own mother. (She does *love* her own mother, I hope?)

Yes, you will change once more; that will be right for you too.

Not handsome — but you could charm the birds out of the trees and send them back up without their feathers!

This friendship is cooling.

You already have.

He is away not through choice but through circumstance, and will return when he can.

The Oracle says yes — practice makes perfect, after all.

Not if they can help it.

You will live for a time in a country separated from your native land by a strip of water.

Yes — but perhaps not in the country of your birth.

The Oracle

Oh yes, my dear! They will!

Too interfering, but a friend in need.

You are not exerting your little self enough at the moment.

No! Her motives are of the highest — which is more than I can say for you, master!

Perhaps — but if you want to know whom he loves best in the world, watch him look in a mirror!

Become a virgin!

Yes, you could not endure the upheaval.

Decisions, decisions. You will choose neither, in the end.

It will need some very specialised assistance to make this dream come true!

Alas! No.

Take care! Remember, if it does, it ends in tears!

The Oracle
Page 67

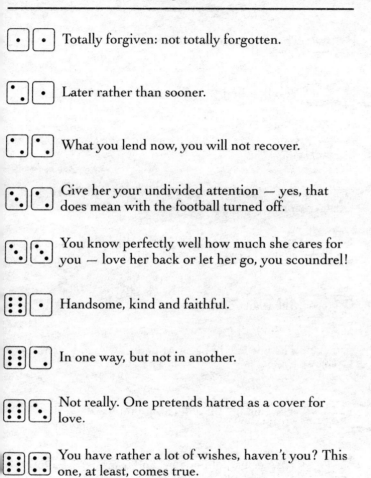

Totally forgiven: not totally forgotten.

Later rather than sooner.

What you lend now, you will not recover.

Give her your undivided attention — yes, that does mean with the football turned off.

You know perfectly well how much she cares for you — love her back or let her go, you scoundrel!

Handsome, kind and faithful.

In one way, but not in another.

Not really. One pretends hatred as a cover for love.

You have rather a lot of wishes, haven't you? This one, at least, comes true.

The most valuable thing to be stolen from you is an idea: remember that.

It should never have happened — stop!

The Oracle
Page 68

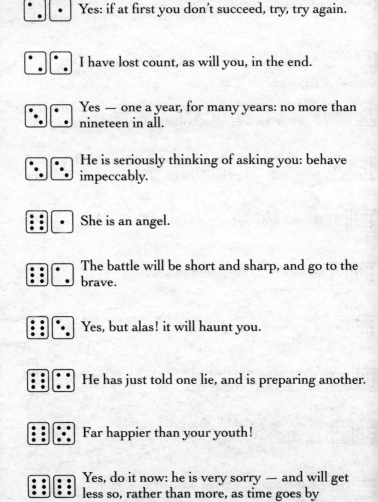

That you have a heart of gold.

Yes: if at first you don't succeed, try, try again.

I have lost count, as will you, in the end.

Yes — one a year, for many years: no more than nineteen in all.

He is seriously thinking of asking you: behave impeccably.

She is an angel.

The battle will be short and sharp, and go to the brave.

Yes, but alas! it will haunt you.

He has just told one lie, and is preparing another.

Far happier than your youth!

Yes, do it now: he is very sorry — and will get less so, rather than more, as time goes by

The Oracle
Page 69

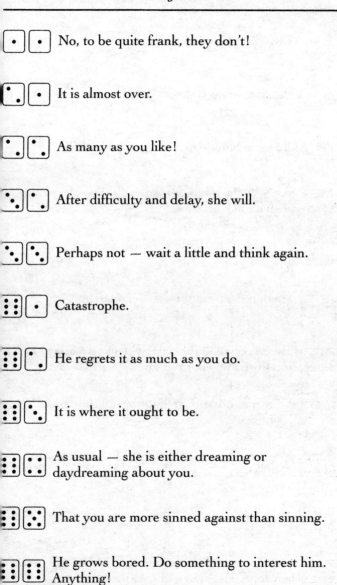

No, to be quite frank, they don't!

It is almost over.

As many as you like!

After difficulty and delay, she will.

Perhaps not — wait a little and think again.

Catastrophe.

He regrets it as much as you do.

It is where it ought to be.

As usual — she is either dreaming or daydreaming about you.

That you are more sinned against than sinning.

He grows bored. Do something to interest him. Anything!

The Oracle
Page 70

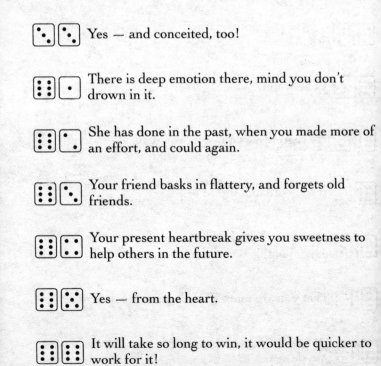

⚀⚀ It will be a long time in coming.

⚁⚀ The wife — and a fine figure of a man she cuts!

⚂⚂ That you will do nicely if guided by her.

⚃⚃ You will make big, black headlines — but for *what*, we ask ourselves?

⚄⚄ Yes — and conceited, too!

⚅⚀ There is deep emotion there, mind you don't drown in it.

⚅⚁ She has done in the past, when you made more of an effort, and could again.

⚅⚂ Your friend basks in flattery, and forgets old friends.

⚅⚃ Your present heartbreak gives you sweetness to help others in the future.

⚅⚄ Yes — from the heart.

⚅⚅ It will take so long to win, it would be quicker to work for it!

The Oracle
Page 71

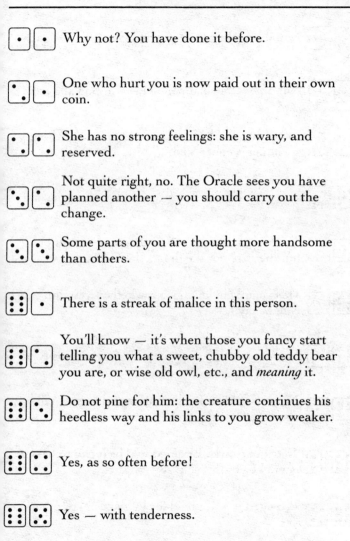

Why not? You have done it before.

One who hurt you is now paid out in their own coin.

She has no strong feelings: she is wary, and reserved.

Not quite right, no. The Oracle sees you have planned another — you should carry out the change.

Some parts of you are thought more handsome than others.

There is a streak of malice in this person.

You'll know — it's when those you fancy start telling you what a sweet, chubby old teddy bear you are, or wise old owl, etc., and *meaning* it.

Do not pine for him: the creature continues his heedless way and his links to you grow weaker.

Yes, as so often before!

Yes — with tenderness.

You will be something of a gypsy: you will live in many different locations for short periods of time.

The Oracle
Page 72

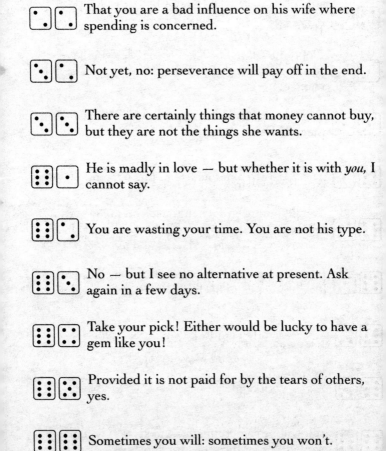

Not unless they are complete fools!

Not unless they happen to be vomiting at 2 a.m.

That you are a bad influence on his wife where spending is concerned.

Not yet, no: perseverance will pay off in the end.

There are certainly things that money cannot buy, but they are not the things she wants.

He is madly in love — but whether it is with *you*, I cannot say.

You are wasting your time. You are not his type.

No — but I see no alternative at present. Ask again in a few days.

Take your pick! Either would be lucky to have a gem like you!

Provided it is not paid for by the tears of others, yes.

Sometimes you will: sometimes you won't.

The Oracle
Page 73

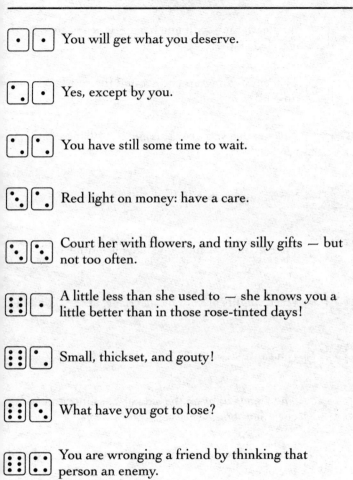

You will get what you deserve.

Yes, except by you.

You have still some time to wait.

Red light on money: have a care.

Court her with flowers, and tiny silly gifts — but not too often.

A little less than she used to — she knows you a little better than in those rose-tinted days!

Small, thickset, and gouty!

What have you got to lose?

You are wronging a friend by thinking that person an enemy.

Well . . . I suppose so . . . but you won't like it, you know.

A little something will be stolen from you, but only to be held as a love token by one who adores you!

The Oracle
Page 74

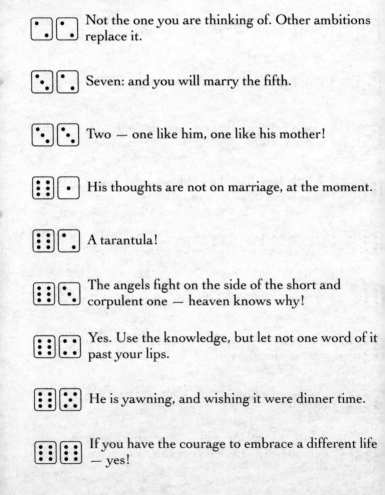

Single, though with much experience of the married state!

That they can wrap you around their little fingers!

Not the one you are thinking of. Other ambitions replace it.

Seven: and you will marry the fifth.

Two — one like him, one like his mother!

His thoughts are not on marriage, at the moment.

A tarantula!

The angels fight on the side of the short and corpulent one — heaven knows why!

Yes. Use the knowledge, but let not one word of it past your lips.

He is yawning, and wishing it were dinner time.

If you have the courage to embrace a different life — yes!

The Oracle
Page 75

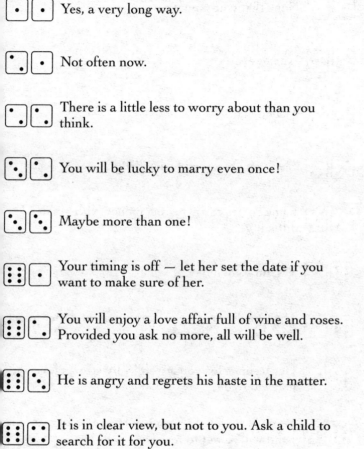

⚀⚀ Yes, a very long way.

⚁⚀ Not often now.

⚂⚂ There is a little less to worry about than you think.

⚃⚃ You will be lucky to marry even once!

⚄⚄ Maybe more than one!

⚅⚀ Your timing is off — let her set the date if you want to make sure of her.

⚅⚁ You will enjoy a love affair full of wine and roses. Provided you ask no more, all will be well.

⚅⚄ He is angry and regrets his haste in the matter.

⚅⚅ It is in clear view, but not to you. Ask a child to search for it for you.

⚅⚄ She is having a deeply interesting, long, telephone conversation, for which someone else will pay. How I hope it isn't you!

⚅⚅ Everyone on planet Earth loves you!

The Oracle
Page 76

None that you cannot carry.

Late, if ever.

Macho man!

That you are a very lucky girl!

Fame comes easily to you, money with greater difficulty.

Yes, on a good day.

The Oracle sees this as a situation far easier to get into than to get out of.

Her feelings for you are still very strong: love and hate alternate.

You will soon hear from your friend, and your mind will be put to rest.

Your heartbreak will soon leave you, and pass to one who deserves it.

They do when you think of them.

The Oracle
Page 77

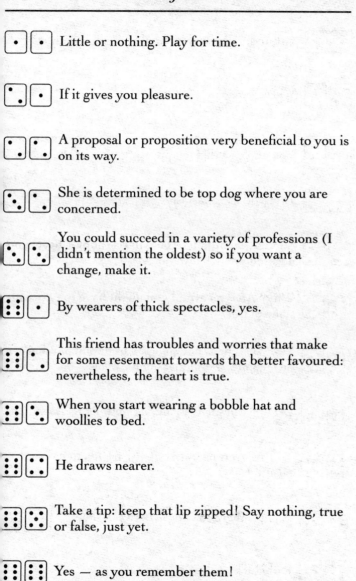

Little or nothing. Play for time.

If it gives you pleasure.

A proposal or proposition very beneficial to you is on its way.

She is determined to be top dog where you are concerned.

You could succeed in a variety of professions (I didn't mention the oldest) so if you want a change, make it.

By wearers of thick spectacles, yes.

This friend has troubles and worries that make for some resentment towards the better favoured: nevertheless, the heart is true.

When you start wearing a bobble hat and woollies to bed.

He draws nearer.

Take a tip: keep that lip zipped! Say nothing, true or false, just yet.

Yes — as you remember them!

The Oracle

A thunderclap will burst above your head.

Yes, some do.

It can be quite difficult to exchange a romantic look across a dirty nappy, but one can always try.

That you are a fascist!

Success eventually. You will rise above those who now tell you what to do.

Why? Are you afraid you might have to part with some of it?

Yes: when he is not engaged in thinking of his own comforts and making his plans.

Let him pursue you, and do nothing to assist him.

You are fretting exceedingly: try to alter your position.

What is there to choose between them?

Lady luck smiles on you. Yes!

The Oracle
Page 79

⚀ ⚀   Because she is more interested in him than you are — or appears to be. Wake up, dear!

⚁ ⚀   So much, that you will not know what to do with it!

⚁ ⚁   Most of the time, yes.

⚂ ⚁   If you are moving away from the centre of a town, yes: if not, no.

⚂ ⚂   No warnings.

⚅ ⚀   A diamond ring would be nice.

⚅ ⚁   She is fickle: if you love her, keep her close to you in the early days, and she will grow to be as constant as the pole star.

⚅ ⚂   Without great good looks or money, but with the charm of the devil.

⚅ ⚃   If in love, think forward one year before deciding.

⚅ ⚄   You will make a lot of enemies in your lifetime, but they trouble you no more than the flittering flies.

⚅ ⚅   You will have your wish within a three: three days, three weeks, three months, or three years.

The Oracle
Page 80

You will see your children's children.

You will be wife, or ex-wife.

That you are an alien!

Yes, you can: but as in all things, you pay a price.

As many as you want, for as long as you want.

Yes, more than one.

If he doesn't ask you, ask him!

She is a small and sturdy daughter of Ireland.

This battle should not be fought between persons, but between one person and his or her iniquities.

If you insist, you will: but you will pay for knowledge in tears.

He is eating something that is bad for him, at a cosy table for two.

The Oracle

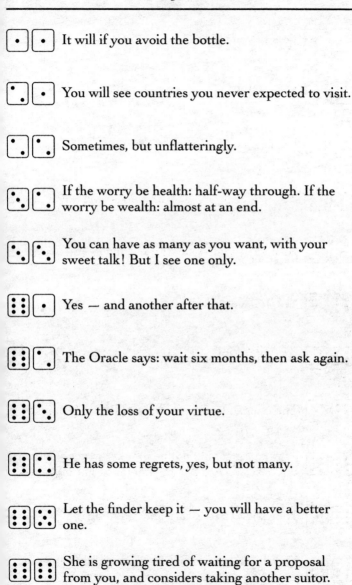

It will if you avoid the bottle.

You will see countries you never expected to visit.

Sometimes, but unflatteringly.

If the worry be health: half-way through. If the worry be wealth: almost at an end.

You can have as many as you want, with your sweet talk! But I see one only.

Yes — and another after that.

The Oracle says: wait six months, then ask again.

Only the loss of your virtue.

He has some regrets, yes, but not many.

Let the finder keep it — you will have a better one.

She is growing tired of waiting for a proposal from you, and considers taking another suitor.

The Oracle

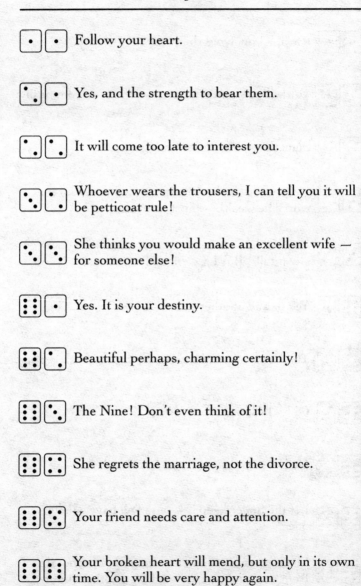

⚀ ⚀	Follow your heart.
⚁ ⚀	Yes, and the strength to bear them.
⚁ ⚁	It will come too late to interest you.
⚂ ⚁	Whoever wears the trousers, I can tell you it will be petticoat rule!
⚂ ⚂	She thinks you would make an excellent wife — for someone else!
⚅ ⚀	Yes. It is your destiny.
⚅ ⚁	Beautiful perhaps, charming certainly!
⚅ ⚂	The Nine! Don't even think of it!
⚅ ⚃	She regrets the marriage, not the divorce.
⚅ ⚄	Your friend needs care and attention.
⚅ ⚅	Your broken heart will mend, but only in its own time. You will be very happy again.

The Oracle

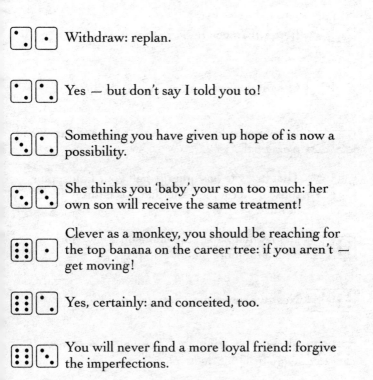 Half as long again as it has already lasted.

Withdraw: replan.

Yes — but don't say I told you to!

Something you have given up hope of is now a possibility.

She thinks you 'baby' your son too much: her own son will receive the same treatment!

Clever as a monkey, you should be reaching for the top banana on the career tree: if you aren't — get moving!

Yes, certainly: and conceited, too.

You will never find a more loyal friend: forgive the imperfections.

At 97 years of age, temporarily, whilst afflicted by boils.

He will return after many days: the parting must be borne.

Needs must, when the devil drives!

The Oracle
Page 84

Yes, of course you will.

Better than you deserve.

Only if you are unconscious at the time.

Not if you hand them over to a fleet of nannies, from birth.

That his wife has inherited all your faults, plus those of her father, and that it is entirely your fault.

Get ready to open the doors on a new horizon, with a lot more money and prestige.

Now whatever gave you *that* idea?

Slightly, occasionally, when he can tear himself away from his many pleasures.

You need do nothing: he is attracted already.

As soon as it can be managed, you would be better to part company.

Do not trouble yourself about it: the choice will be made for you.

The Oracle
Page 85

⚀ ⚀ No!

⚁ ⚀ Novelty, my dear.

⚁ ⚁ Greed is not attractive, my beady-eyed one; do try not to let it show.

⚂ ⚂ It is sometimes still held against you.

⚂ ⚂ I see a removal van, outside a house screened by trees. If this is your present or next home, a move is imminent.

⚃ ⚀ Take care on heights at present.

⚃ ⚁ Flirt with her — and play just a little hard to get.

⚃ ⚂ She has not yet given you her whole heart.

⚃ ⚃ Many to choose from — they whirl like snowflakes; but the Oracle selects a tall young man with light brown hair, and perhaps glasses.

⚃ ⚄ Yes, you should.

⚅ ⚅ One only wishes you ill: you know why.

The Oracle
Page 86

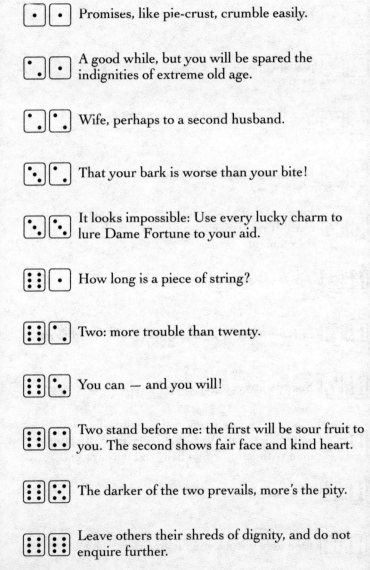

Promises, like pie-crust, crumble easily.

A good while, but you will be spared the indignities of extreme old age.

Wife, perhaps to a second husband.

That your bark is worse than your bite!

It looks impossible: Use every lucky charm to lure Dame Fortune to your aid.

How long is a piece of string?

Two: more trouble than twenty.

You can — and you will!

Two stand before me: the first will be sour fruit to you. The second shows fair face and kind heart.

The darker of the two prevails, more's the pity.

Leave others their shreds of dignity, and do not enquire further.

The Oracle
Page 87

⚀ ⚀ Not him!

⚁ ⚀ You have a strong constitution, but take care not to abuse it.

⚁ ⚁ Yes, but not to the place you are thinking of.

⚂ ⚂ Yes, affectionately.

⚃ ⚃ It continues for some time.

⚅ ⚀ You will have two husbands.

⚅ ⚁ A longed-for baby will arrive for her.

⚅ ⚃ Are you mad? Do you mock the oracle? Deep in your heart, you already know the answer to this.

⚅ ⚃ Nothing, if you are wise.

⚅ ⚄ Only the manner in which it was done.

⚅ ⚅ Someone knows, and could tell, if they chose.

The Oracle
Page 88

⚀⚀ Certainly *not!*

⚁⚀ Let head rule heart in this.

⚁⚁ Not too many.

⚂⚂ Very soon, or not at all.

⚂⚂ You will!

⚅⚀ She thinks you a sweet, malleable little thing — which just shows what a clever girl you are!

⚅⚀ During a ten-year period of your life, you will know fame.

⚅⚂ Well now, that depends — but I can tell you that to at least one person, you are.

⚅⚁ Put this question to her husband or to your wife, if you have one, then you can know for sure.

⚅⚂ She thinks herself mad to have to let you go!

⚅⚅ Your friend is busy, and happy.

The Oracle
Page 89

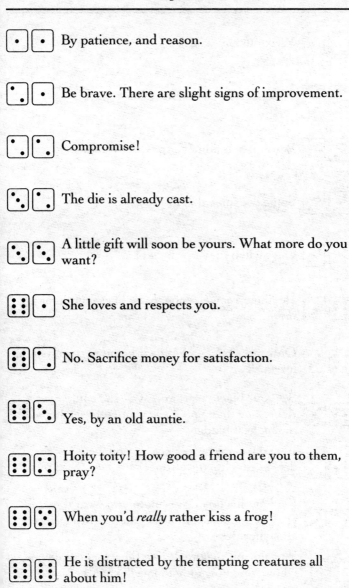

By patience, and reason.

Be brave. There are slight signs of improvement.

Compromise!

The die is already cast.

A little gift will soon be yours. What more do you want?

She loves and respects you.

No. Sacrifice money for satisfaction.

Yes, by an old auntie.

Hoity toity! How good a friend are you to them, pray?

When you'd *really* rather kiss a frog!

He is distracted by the tempting creatures all about him!

Yes: you may win.

Patience relieves sorrow, you'll see.

Better it should never be discovered.

Some do: some don't.

Only when they are awake!

He likes you well enough: he likes your cooking more!

Only after bone-aching work and nerve-crushing insecurity.

Set your black heart at rest — she could pick a richer one than you if she wanted to sell herself to the highest bidder.

If he dips into his pocket for you, he does: the deeper the dip, the stronger the love, with this fellow!

Find out his favourite colour and wear it, provided it does not make you look whey-faced and charmless.

You consult the oracle as a time-wasting device, when you know only too well what the answer will be!

The Oracle
Page 91

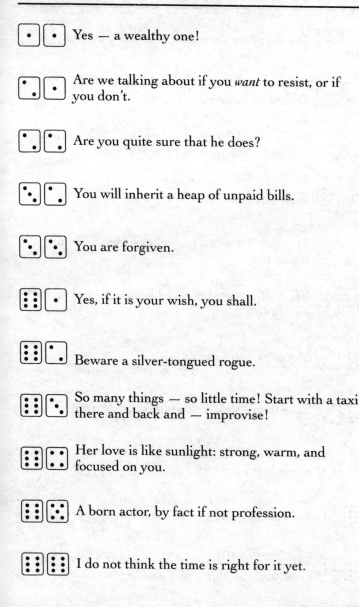

Yes — a wealthy one!

Are we talking about if you *want* to resist, or if you don't.

Are you quite sure that he does?

You will inherit a heap of unpaid bills.

You are forgiven.

Yes, if it is your wish, you shall.

Beware a silver-tongued rogue.

So many things — so little time! Start with a taxi there and back and — improvise!

Her love is like sunlight: strong, warm, and focused on you.

A born actor, by fact if not profession.

I do not think the time is right for it yet.

The Oracle

No. Serpentine cunning will win the day.

A promise will be kept, and something else, not promised, be given.

At the age of 79 years your teeth will be renewed, and you will have some use of them.

Widow.

That you are much better at giving advice than at taking it.

Yes — if you are prepared for much work and sacrifice.

More than you should!

Two: then a welcome addition years later.

Your question is not sincere, since in any case you are only toying with him.

Her face is pretty: her temper less so.

Neither. The battle will be waged in a storm of tears, and the object of it will be lost.

The Oracle
Page 93

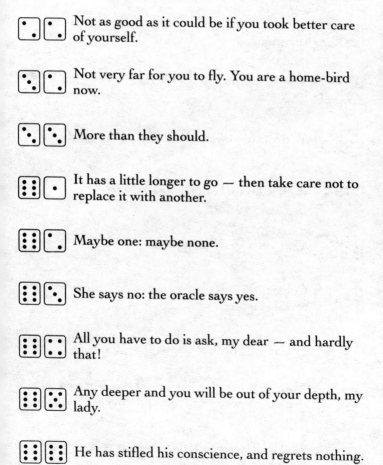

⚀⚀ If you play your hand cleverly, you will.

⚁⚀ He will appear to, when it suits him.

⚁⚁ Not as good as it could be if you took better care of yourself.

⚂⚀ Not very far for you to fly. You are a home-bird now.

⚂⚂ More than they should.

⚃⚀ It has a little longer to go — then take care not to replace it with another.

⚃⚁ Maybe one: maybe none.

⚃⚂ She says no: the oracle says yes.

⚄⚄ All you have to do is ask, my dear — and hardly that!

⚄⚄ Any deeper and you will be out of your depth, my lady.

⚅⚅ He has stifled his conscience, and regrets nothing.

The Oracle

⚀ ⚀   Resist temptation!

⚁ ⚀   Above all, not to them!

⚁ ⚁   'East or West, home's best'. Apply this to your situation.

⚂ ⚁   You will always find willing hands to carry them for you.

⚂ ⚂   Two lots of news on the same day . . . and soon.

⚅ ⚀   Both want to: both try to: disaster!

⚅ ⚁   That you can do no wrong!

⚅ ⚂   Come now, don't be modest — you already are in certain circles!

⚅ ⚃   You are the belle of the ball!

⚅ ⚄   Nothing much. It's like one of those fireworks that go out when you light the blue touch paper and retire.

⚅ ⚅   That rather depends on what she is doing, and who she is doing it with.

The Oracle
Page 95

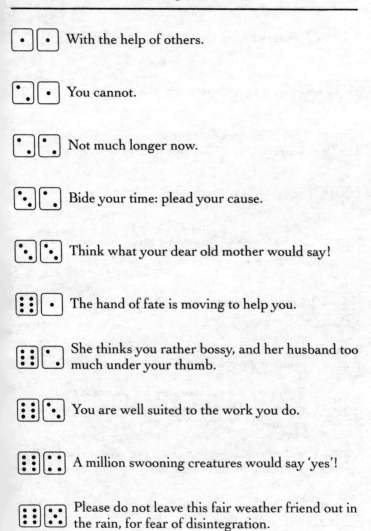

⚀⚀ With the help of others.

⚁⚀ You cannot.

⚁⚁ Not much longer now.

⚂⚂ Bide your time: plead your cause.

⚂⚂ Think what your dear old mother would say!

⚅⚀ The hand of fate is moving to help you.

⚅⚁ She thinks you rather bossy, and her husband too much under your thumb.

⚅⚂ You are well suited to the work you do.

⚅⚅ A million swooning creatures would say 'yes'!

⚅⚅ Please do not leave this fair weather friend out in the rain, for fear of disintegration.

⚅⚅ When it's winter in your heart.

The Oracle
Page 96

⚁ ⚀ That depends what you are trying to forget!

⚁ ⚀ Why give up before the battle is fought?

⚁ ⚁ These things take time: everything passes, even pain. You will be happy again one day.

⚂ ⚁ I shudder to think!

⚂ ⚂ Sometimes, when you wheedle their secrets out of them!

⚅ ⚀ Oh yes, from the very start!

⚅ ⚀ His thoughts are as impenetrable as fog: ask me again in a week's time.

⚅ ⚂ If you are not yet working for yourself, you should be. Double harness is best, so find a partner.

⚅ ⚁ If she does, it is your own fault. What else have you taken pains to offer her?

⚅ ⚄ His love is growing and opening like a rose in the sun.

⚅ ⚅ Enlist the help of a mutual friend, who will arrange as many 'accidental' meetings as possible, without arousing his suspicions.

⚁ ⚀ Yes — be kind.

⚁ ⚀ A would-be one, who does not interest him.

⚁ ⚁ You are making a joke, madam!

⚂ ⚁ Because he thinks they are two of a kind.

⚃ ⚃ A little money, a lot of arguments.

⚅ ⚀ If it is not, it ought to be.

⚅ ⚁ Maybe not for quite a long time.

⚅ ⚂ Famine and feast, alternating. Be careful at work.

⚅ ⚄ Ask her to marry you — that's usually a great pleaser.

⚅ ⚄ She would love you more if you returned her love equally, and offered her more entertainment.

⚅ ⚅ A dark-haired rogue, much given to drinking and debauching.

The Oracle
Page 98

⚀ ⚀ Tilted against you.

⚁ ⚀ Yes, but in private.

⚁ ⚁ If you wish this promise to be kept, you must apply yourself to making sure that it is.

⚂ ⚁ If you avoid perils by poison and by deep water, you will.

⚂ ⚂ Married — which will be a big surprise to some.

⚃ ⚀ That you have champagne tastes, and beer money.

⚃ ⚁ If you do, it will be when you pass the age of 42.

⚃ ⚂ A baker's dozen — and in the last you will meet your match.

⚃ ⚃ One only — a loved child born late.

⚃ ⚄ Yes, if you are patient.

⚃ ⚅ A tiger in pussy-cat's clothing!

The Oracle

The years of the early family life.

By luck, you will.

Leopards don't change their spots — nor dogs their tricks!

Good, except for a tendency to chest complaints.

Not quite as far as you would wish or hope.

No. They talk of nothing of importance!

Are you worrying about something that cannot be changed? Time solves all problems.

Only one, your heart's darling!

No more, except by stealth!

If you are holding this book in your left hand, the answer is yes.

Live today, pay tomorrow — you have been warned!

The Oracle
Page 100

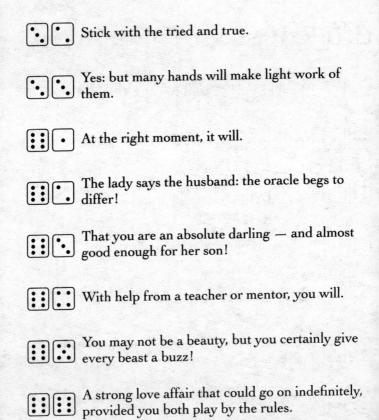

Little or no change.

Alter your list of priorities.

Confession is good for the soul, they say: confess to somebody else.

Stick with the tried and true.

Yes: but many hands will make light work of them.

At the right moment, it will.

The lady says the husband: the oracle begs to differ!

That you are an absolute darling — and almost good enough for her son!

With help from a teacher or mentor, you will.

You may not be a beauty, but you certainly give every beast a buzz!

A strong love affair that could go on indefinitely, provided you both play by the rules.

The Oracle is silent!

for

darkness doth prevail

and

The Children of Men

are forbidden

to inquire further!

MADAME MARIE

is a well-known clairvoyant whose advice is sought by people from all walks of life. She has inherited her 'second sight' from her mother's Highland forebears and had her first psychic 'flash' as a child, when she was taken to watch the Grand National at Aintree and predicted the winner – an outsider at 100–1. She now lives and works in north-west London.